ANNABEL KARMEL

Children's First COOKBOOK

Have fun in the kitchen!

LONDON, NEW YORK, MUNICH,
MELBOURNE, and DELHI

LONDON, NEW YORK, MUNICH,
MELBOURNE, and DELHI

SENIOR ART EDITOR • Claire Patané
SENIOR EDITOR • Elinor Greenwood
DESIGNER • Sadie Thomas
PHOTOGRAPHER • Dave King
FOOD STYLISTS • Dagmar Vesely,
Caroline Mason

PUBLISHING MANAGER • Sue Leonard
MANAGING ART EDITOR • Clare Shedden
JACKET DESIGNER • Victoria Harvey
PRODUCTION • Alison Lenane
DTP DESIGNER • Almudena Díaz

First published in Great Britain in 2005 by
Dorling Kindersley Limited
80 Strand, London WC2R 0RL

A Penguin Company

8 10 9

Copyright © 2005 Dorling Kindersley Limited,
London
Text copyright © 2005 Annabel Karmel

A catalogue record for this book
is available from the British Library

ISBN-13: 978-1-4053-0843-4

Colour reproduction by Colourscan
Printed and bound in China by SNP Leefung

Discover more at
www.dk.com

Contents

This is my first book for children. I have chosen recipes that are fun, look and taste fabulous, yet are easy enough for cooks as young as three years old to make.

Children love to cook and relish kneading and rolling out dough or cracking eggs. Cooking with your child is a terrific way of bonding. Also, they learn skills like counting, measuring, weighing, and understanding time – all without noticing it.

In this book there are lots of healthy recipes for dips, main meals, and smoothies, as well as yummy puddings. Children will eagerly tuck into something they have prepared themselves, and take great pride in watching someone else enjoy their food. Also, getting children involved in the kitchen is a great way to motivate fussy eaters.

Take time to cook with your child and, above all, have fun in the kitchen!

Annabel Karmel

Things you will need:

Mixing bowl	Knife and fork	Small saucepan	Wooden spoon	Large bowl	Wooden spatula
Sieve	Glasses	Clingfilm	Rolling pin	Baking tray	Masher
Bun tins	Paper cake cases	Cookie cutter	Cooling rack	Piping bag	Palette knife

Things you will do:

beat   mix   cream   grate   mash

melt   puree   sift   simmer   whisk

How to knead:

1. Flatten your dough slightly, then fold it over towards you.

2. Press the heels of your hands into the dough and push the dough slightly away from you.

3. Turn the dough through ¼ turn, then fold, press, and turn again. Repeat for about 8 minutes.

Frying pan

Cheese grater

Saucepan with lid

Whisk

Wok

Brush

Square cake tin

Blender

Round cake tin

Straws and skewers

Lolly moulds

Tall glasses

What things mean:

1. Basic equipment you'll need to make a recipe.

2. Number of people served or things made.

3. An adult needs to help with this step.

It's time to get cracking and cook some eggs.

sunny scrambled eggs

Simply scramble eggs for
a bright start to the day.

You will need:

2 eggs

15 g (½ oz)
butter

salt and
pepper

2 tbsp
milk

How to make it...

1 Crack the eggs by tapping the shells on the rim of a bowl. Then split the eggs open.

2 Whisk the eggs together with a pinch of salt and pepper.

3 Melt the butter over a medium heat. Pour in the eggs and milk and keep stirring.

4 Two minutes later, when the mixture has thickened and looks set, spoon it onto a plate.

Serve buttery 'rays' of toast around your egg.

my favourite pancakes

A foolproof pancake batter – no flops when you flip these!

You will need:

a big pinch of salt

strawberries

blueberries

raspberries

maple syrup

90 ml (3 fl oz) water

125 g (4 oz) plain flour

2 eggs

200 ml (7 fl oz) milk

60 g (2 oz) butter

How to make them...

1 **Sift the flour** and salt into a mixing bowl. Then make a well in the centre of the flour.

2 **Break the eggs** into the well. Whisk the eggs and flour together. Next mix together the water and milk in a separate bowl or jug.

3 **Add the liquid** to the flour, a little at a time, whisking to make a smooth batter. Melt 2 tbsp of the butter and stir it into the batter. Sieve if lumpy.

4 **Melt butter** in a small frying pan – just use enough to coat the bottom of the pan.

5 **Add the batter** – you'll need about 2 tbsp for each pancake. Tilt the pan so the batter covers the base.

6 **Cook the pancake** for about one minute. Use a spatula to loosen it, then flip it over! Cook the second side for 30 seconds.

7 **Fill the pancakes** with fresh fruit and plenty of maple syrup.

slurpy spaghetti

Serve with tomato sauce and get your taste buds zinging.

You will need:

2 tbsp olive oil

½ tbsp tomato puree

½ tsp balsamic vinegar

½ tsp sugar

400 g (14 oz) tin of chopped tomatoes

1 onion, peeled and chopped

200 g (7 oz) spaghetti

1 clove garlic, crushed

salt and pepper

Parmesan cheese

How to make it...

1 **Heat the oil in a pan.**
Add the onion and garlic and fry for 5 minutes or until the onion is see-through and soft.

2 **Add the tinned tomatoes,**
tomato puree, balsamic vinegar, sugar, and a pinch of salt and pepper. Cover with a lid and simmer for about 20 minutes.

3 Cook the spaghetti in a large pan of boiling water. Check the packet to see how long to cook it.

4 Grate the Parmesan cheese, keeping your fingers safely away from the grater! Drain the pasta, put it into bowls, and top with the tomato sauce.

Sprinkle with the grated cheese and get slurping!

perfect pasta

Pass the pasta! This dish is quick and easy to prepare.

You will need:

4 tbsp honey

2 tbsp rice vinegar

2 tbsp of soy sauce

1 tbsp sesame oil

2 cooked chicken breasts

150 g (5 oz) sweetcorn

2 spring onions

175 g (6 oz) broccoli

200 g (7 oz) pasta shapes

How to make it...

1 **Cook the pasta shapes** according to the packet instructions. Add the broccoli for the last 3 minutes.

2 **Shred the cooked chicken** into bite-sized pieces. Remove any bits of skin.

3 Carefully slice the spring onions.

4 Make a dressing by mixing together the honey, vinegar, soy sauce, and sesame oil.

5 Mix together the pasta, broccoli, chicken, spring onions, sweetcorn, and the dressing.

6 Serve it out. Your pasta salad is now ready to eat.

2 in 1

Learn to make
pizza dough,
then two top
toppings...

pizza
dough

You will need:

1½ tsp dried yeast

1 tsp sugar

2 tbsp olive oil, plus extra for oiling

250 ml (8 fl oz) warm water

375 g (13 oz) strong plain flour, plus extra for sprinkling

salt and pepper

How to make it...

1 Mix the yeast with 3 tbsp water. Set this aside for 10 minutes or until it is frothy.

2 Sift the flour into a bowl and add the sugar, salt and pepper. Then dig a well in the centre.

3 Pour the yeast, water, and oil into the well. Use your hands to mix everything together.

4 Sprinkle flour over a clean work surface. Then knead the dough for 8 minutes, until it is smooth and elastic.

5 Oil a large bowl, pop in the dough, and cover with clingfilm. Leave in a warm place until the dough has doubled in size.

6 Is it ready? Poke holes in the dough. If the holes remain, it's ready. Punch down with your fists and place on a floured surface.

2 in 1 pizzas

Get arty with your pizzas and make them look like faces.
Or add chicken for a finger licking feast.

You will need:

your pizza dough

pizza sauce or passata

diced ham

sweet peppers

mushrooms

sliced pitted olives

grated cheese

cherry tomatoes

basil

1 cooked chicken breast, diced

pepperoni

spring onions

How to make them...

1 **Knead the dough again.**
Then cut it into four equal pieces.
Roll each piece into an 18 cm/7 in circle
and place on a baking sheet.

2 **Preheat the oven**
to 220°C/425° F (Gas mark 7).
Spread pizza sauce or passata on each
pizza base.

3 **Make faces** on your pizzas using your favourite toppings. Try tomato noses, olive eyes, sweet pepper hair, or any other combination.

4 **Spoon chicken,** sliced spring onions and sweet peppers onto your pizzas for an alternative treat.

5 **Sprinkle cheese** all over your pizzas. Then cook them in the oven for 12 minutes or until golden and bubbling.

mice in jackets

These baked potato mice are almost too gorgeous to eat!

You will need:

radishes

cherry tomatoes

spring onions

chives

raisins

salt and pepper

4 potatoes

1 tbsp oil

5 tbsp milk

60 g (2 oz) grated cheese

30 g (1 oz) butter

How to make them...

1 Wash the potatoes and pat them dry. Prick the skins with a fork and put the potatoes on a baking tray. Brush them all over with oil.

2 Bake the potatoes until they are soft. Medium-sized potatoes take about one hour in an oven heated to 200°C/400°F (gas mark 6).

3 Cool enough to handle? Then cut off the tops and carefully scoop out the soft potato centres. You can throw away the lids (or eat them).

4 Mash the soft centres with the butter, milk, three quarters of the cheese, salt and pepper. Then pop the mixture back into the potato jackets.

5 Sprinkle the remaining cheese on the potatoes and cook under the grill for a few minutes until golden.

6 Make a nose and whiskers with half a tomato held in place with a cocktail stick and chives tucked behind.

7 Finish decorating with raisin eyes, radish ears, and spring onion tails.

sweet and sour chicken

This recipe is a great favourite and it always looks lovely and colourful.

You will need:

250 g (8 oz) diced chicken breast

75 g (2 ½ oz) carrot matchsticks

60 g (2 oz) sliced baby corn

2 tbsp sliced spring onions

4 tbsp vegetable oil

200 g (7 oz) white rice

60 g (2 oz) trimmed green beans

Batter:

1 egg yolk

black pepper

1 ½ tbsp cornflour

1 tbsp milk

Sauce:

1 tbsp soy sauce

4 tbsp chicken stock

2 tbsp rice wine vinegar

2 tbsp tomato ketchup

2 tbsp caster sugar

How to make it...

1 Start cooking the rice according to the instructions on the packet.

2 Make the sauce by mixing together all the sauce ingredients in a bowl.

3 Beat together the batter ingredients in another bowl.

4 **Dip the chicken** in the batter, then fry it in 2 tbsp oil. Remove from the pan and set aside.

5 **Next stir-fry** the carrots, baby corn, and beans in the remaining 2 tbsp oil for 4 minutes.

6 **Add the sauce** and boil for 1 minute. Then add the chicken and spring onions and heat through.

7 **Serve it out.** Spoon a helping of sweet and sour chicken on top of a bed of rice.

avocado frog dip

Cause a stir with this froggy dip. Choose your favourite vegetables to go with it... Gribbit!

You will need:

1 large avocado

1 tomato

1 tbsp of lemon juice

2 tbsp of sour cream

chives

salt and pepper

cucumber slices

stuffed olives

carrot batons

cucumber sticks

strips of pitta bread

red pepper slices

1 Cut the avocado in half, remove the stone from the middle and scoop out the flesh.

2 Squeeze lemon juice onto the avocado to help it keep its colour. One tablespoon is enough.

3 Mash up the avocado and lemon juice and mix it with the sour cream.

4 Chop the tomato into tiny pieces. Snip 1 ½ tbsp chives. Mix these with the mash.

5 Season the dip with a grinding of salt and pepper.

Gribbit!

6 Make a frog face on your dip using sliced cucumber and olives for eyes and chives for a mouth.

fishy fruit dip

Serve this dip with kebabs
of your favourite fruit.

You will need:

1 mango
(or 1 peach)

150 g
(5 oz) Greek
yoghurt

chocolate
chips

mandarin
segments

1 tsp honey

kiwi and apple slices

How to make it...

1 First cut up the mango
by slicing it in half and cutting the
flesh into cubes. Gently turn the skin
inside out. Cut off the cubes.

2 Mash the mango
in a bowl. Use a fork or potato
masher to make the mango into a
smooth pulp.

3 Mix the mango
with the Greek yoghurt and honey to sweeten.

4 Decorate the dip
with a mandarin mouth, chocolate chip eye, and kiwi fruit and apple fins and tail.

5 Make fruity dip sticks
by threading chunks of your favourite fruits onto skewers. Then get dipping!

melon

grapes

strawberries

pineapple

easy peasy cupcakes

Soft, spongy cupcakes – they're as easy as...

1

2

3.

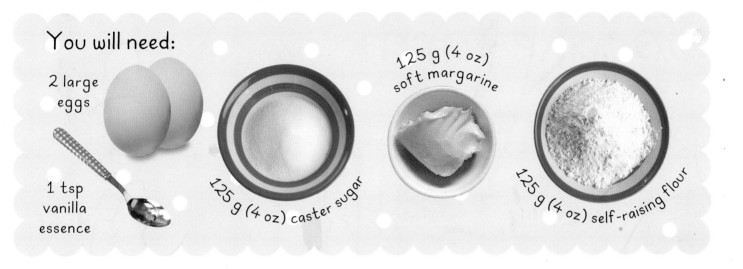

You will need:

2 large eggs

1 tsp vanilla essence

125 g (4 oz) caster sugar

125 g (4 oz) soft margarine

125 g (4 oz) self-raising flour

How to make them...

1 **Heat the oven** to 180°C/350°F (gas 4). Put all the ingredients in a bowl and beat them together until the mixture is smooth and lighter in colour.

2 **Line a bun tin** with paper cake cases and half fill each case with the cake mixture.

3 **Cook the cakes** for 18 to 20 minutes. You can tell they are done when they have risen up, are golden in colour, and spring back into shape when pressed.

cupcake farm

Decorate your cupcakes and make the sweetest little animals.

You will need:

your cupcakes

250 g (8 oz) icing sugar

biscuits

chocolate buttons

125 g (4 oz) butter, softened

1 tbsp water

marshmallows (including mini marshmallows)

colourful sweets

pink food colouring

tubes of writing icing

1 First make the butter icing.
Sieve the icing sugar into a bowl. In another bowl, beat the butter until creamy. Gradually add the icing sugar to the butter, beating to keep the mixture smooth. Finally, beat in the water.

2 Make marshmallow sheep. Spread a thick layer of butter icing over the top of the cupcakes.

3 Stick on marshmallows, using large ones for faces, halved ones for ears, and mini ones for woolly coats.

4 Make pink piggies by mixing a few drops of food colouring with the butter icing. Spread the pink icing on top of the cupcakes.

5 Stick on a nose made from a large marshmallow and ears made from slices of marshmallow.

6 To make puppy cakes, spread on the icing, then stick on biscuit ears and use sweets for eyes and noses.

7 Draw the faces on your animals using writing icing squeezed from a tube.

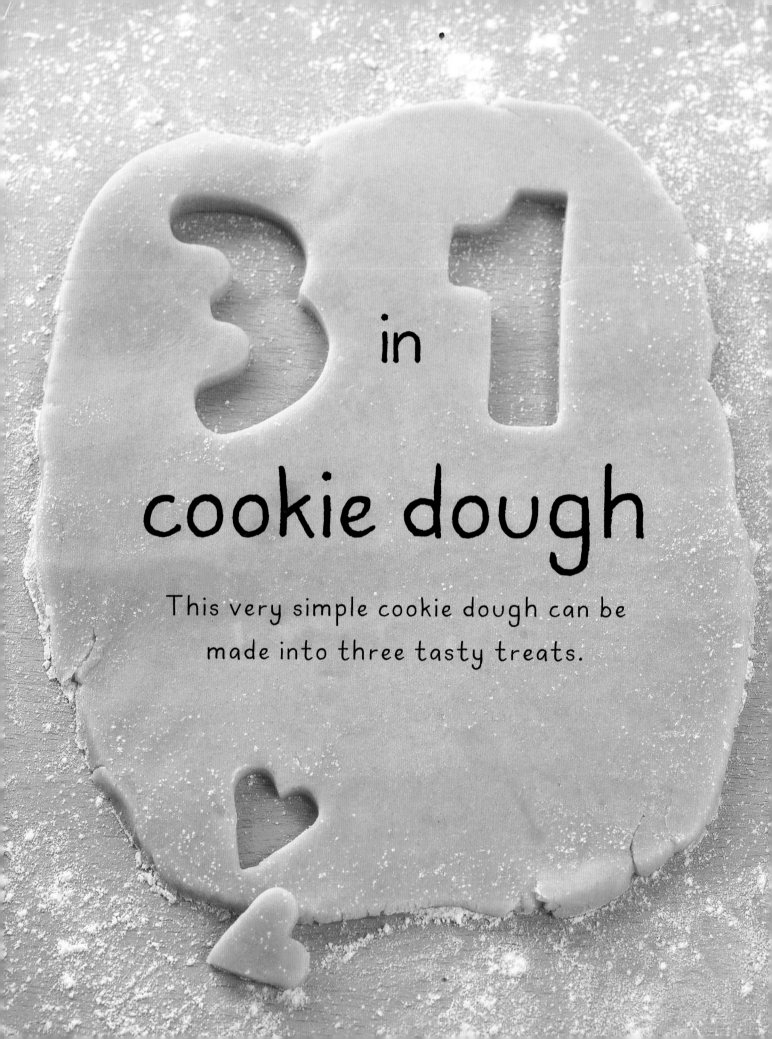

3 1

in

cookie dough

This very simple cookie dough can be made into three tasty treats.

You will need:

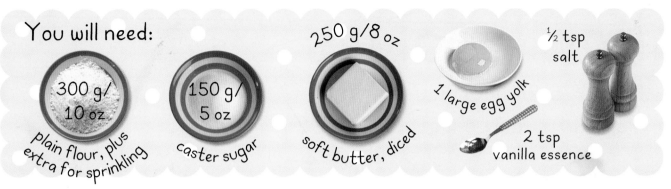

300 g/ 10 oz
plain flour, plus extra for sprinkling

150 g/ 5 oz
caster sugar

250 g/8 oz
soft butter, diced

1 large egg yolk

½ tsp salt

2 tsp vanilla essence

How to make it...

1 **Beat the butter**
and sugar together in a bowl.

2 **Add the egg yolk**
and vanilla essence and beat the mixture until it is smooth.

3 **Next add the flour**
and salt and mix everything together to form a smooth dough.

4 **Mould the dough**
into a ball, wrap it in clingfilm, and leave it in the fridge for 30 minutes.

animal cookies

Here's how to turn your dough
into a crowd of cookie creatures.

You will need:

125 g (4 oz) icing sugar, sifted

1 tbsp water

1 tbsp cocoa powder

writing
icing

your cookie dough

How to make them...

1 Heat the oven
to 180°C/350°F
(gas 4). Divide the dough in
half. Make one half brown by
rubbing in the cocoa powder.

2 Roll the dough
to about ½ cm
(¼ in) thick on a surface
sprinkled with flour.

3 Cut out animals.
Put them on non-stick
or lined baking trays. Roll
out leftover dough and cut
out more animals.

4 **Cook the cookies** for 12 minutes or until golden. Leave them on a wire rack to cool.

5 **Make icing** by mixing together the icing sugar and water. Pipe the icing onto the cookies to decorate.

6 **Draw on faces** and other features using writing icing squeezed from a tube.

Animal cookies are great served with cold milk.

....baa

jam sweethearts

Show someone how much you love them with these scrummy, jammy heart cookies.

You will need:

your cookie dough

60 g (2 oz) softened butter, plus extra for greasing

90 g (3 oz) icing sugar, sifted

jam

a few drops vanilla essence

1 tsp water

How to make them...

1 **Heat the oven** to 180°C/350°F (gas 4). Roll dough to ½ cm (¼ in) thick. Cut out circles with a 6 cm (2 ½ in) cutter.

2 **Arrange circles** on greased baking trays. Cut hearts from half your cookie circles using a 2 cm (1 in) cutter.

3 **Cook the cookies** for 12 minutes or until golden. Leave them to cool completely.

4 Make the butter icing by beating the butter until smooth, then gradually beating in the icing sugar, water, and vanilla essence. Spread butter icing over the whole (not heart) cookies.

5 Now spoon on the jam. Blob a small spoonful of jam on top of the butter icing. Pop the heart cookies on top. Now eat them – they're lovely!

rolled cookies

Roll up! Roll up! Make chocolate and cranberry spirals here!

You will need:

a few drops of pink food colouring

your cookie dough

15 g (½ oz) chopped dried cranberries

1 tbsp cocoa powder

How to make them...

1 **Divide the dough** into four. Colour one piece brown by rubbing in cocoa powder. Colour another pink with cranberries and food colouring. Leave two plain.

2 **Wrap the dough** in clingfilm. Put it in the fridge for about 30 minutes. Preheat the oven to 180°C/350°F (gas mark 4).

3 **Roll the dough** on a floured surface. Each piece of dough should make a rectangle about 18 x 20 cm (7 x 8 in).

4 For rolled cookies place the plain dough on the chocolate dough. Trim the edges and roll into a log. Repeat with the pink dough.

5 Marbled cookies are made from all the dough trimmings. Simply knead them together, then roll them into a log.

6 Slice the logs into ½ cm (¼ in) cookies. Pop the cookies on non-stick or lined baking trays.

7 Now cook your cookies for 15 to 18 minutes or until lightly golden.

chocolate fridge cake

These delicious bricks of chocolate cake
can keep for two weeks in the fridge.

You will need:

250 g (8 oz) digestive biscuits

150 g (5 oz) plain chocolate

150 g (5 oz) golden syrup

150 g (5 oz) milk chocolate

100 g (3 ½ oz) unsalted butter

100 g (3 ½ oz) dried apricots, chopped

75 g (2 ½ oz) raisins

60 g (2 oz) chopped pecans, (optional)

How to make it...

1 **Use clingfilm** to line a 20 cm (8 in) shallow, square-shaped tin. Leave extra clingfilm hanging over the sides.

2 **Bash the biscuits** into pieces using a rolling pin. (Put them in a plastic bag first so they don't go everywhere!)

3 **Melt chocolate,** butter, and golden syrup in a heatproof bowl set over a pan of simmering water. Stir occasionally.

4 Remove the bowl from the heat and stir in the broken biscuits, apricots, raisins, and pecans (optional).

5 Spoon the mix into the tin. Level the surface by pressing it down with a potato masher.

6 Leave to cool, then put the chocolate mixture in the fridge for 1 to 2 hours to set.

7 Turn out the cake and peel off the clingfilm. Cut the cake into 12 squares and enjoy!

raspberry ripple cheesecake

Swirl raspberries and cream to make the dreamiest cheesecake ever!

You will need:

- 125 g (4 oz) butter
- 250 g (8 oz) digestive biscuits
- 1 tsp pure vanilla essence
- 450 g (16 oz) cream cheese
- 225 g (7 ½ oz) caster sugar
- 300 g (10 oz) fresh raspberries
- 60 g (2 oz) icing sugar
- 400 ml (14 fl oz) double cream

How to make it...

1 Put the biscuits in a bag. Then use a rolling pin to roll and crush them into crumbs.

2 Melt the butter in a pan. Tip the crushed biscuits into the butter and stir thoroughly.

3 Line a 20 cm (8 in) cake tin (one with a removable base), with clingfilm. Spoon in the biscuit mixture, press it flat with a masher, and pop it in the fridge.

4 Make raspberry puree by bringing the raspberries and icing sugar to the boil, then simmering for 10 minutes. Cool, then press through a sieve.

5 Mix together
the cream cheese, caster sugar, and vanilla essence. Whip the double cream until stiff, then fold it into the cheese mixture.

6 Spread topping
on the biscuit base – use about ¾ of the cheese mixture. Then blob on ¾ of the puree and swirl it into the cheesecake mixture.

7 Gently spread
on the remaining cheesecake mixture. Drizzle on straight lines of raspberry puree. Pull a skewer across the lines for a feathered effect.

Leave the cheesecake in the fridge for at least 2 hours or overnight.

peach melba shake up

You'll be all shook up with this perfect pick-me-up!

How to make it...

You will need:
400 g (14 oz) peach slices
raspberries 100 g (3 ½ oz)
200 ml (7 fl oz) raspberry drinking yoghurt

1 Get rid of any pips by pressing the raspberries through a sieve.

2 Blend the raspberries, peach (except two slices), and yoghurt. Serve decorated with the reserved peach.

coconut dream

This is a creamy drink with a tropical taste.

You will need:
125 ml (4 fl oz) coconut milk
300 ml (12 fl oz) pineapple juice
2 scoops vanilla ice cream
100 g (3 ½ oz) pineapple

1 First blend then pour.
Put the coconut milk, pineapple juice, ice cream, and pineapple (except two bits) into a blender and whizz. Pour the drink into glasses and serve with the reserved pineapple.

summertime smoothie

This is fruity and refreshing on hot days.

How to make it...

You will need:

2 peaches, sliced

1 banana

60 g (2 oz) strawberries

125 g (4 oz) vanilla yoghurt

125 ml (4 fl oz) orange juice

1 **First prepare the fruit.**
Peel and slice the banana and peaches. Remove the green leaves from most of the strawberries. Cut the strawberries into slices.

2 **Push strawberry slices**
and banana onto straws. Put all the other fruit in a blender and whizz. Pour the drink into glasses and serve with the straws of fruit.

coconut dream

peach melba shake up

summertime smoothie

traffic light lollies

Red, yellow, green –
let's go and eat!

You will need:

3 large ripe peaches

90 g (3 oz) caster sugar

5 large ripe kiwi fruit

¼ small watermelon

3 tbsp water

How to make them...

1 **For the red,** remove the melon seeds. Puree the flesh in a blender, together with 30 g (1 oz) of the sugar. Pour the puree into ice lolly moulds so they are all ⅓ full. Freeze for 1 ½ hours.

2 **For the yellow,** peel the peaches. Blend the flesh, together with 30 g (1 oz) of the sugar. Pour this yellow puree onto the frozen red puree so the lolly moulds are now ⅔ full. Freeze until solid.

3 **For the green,** peel the kiwis. Blend the flesh, together with the water and 30 g (1 oz) sugar. Press the puree through a sieve to get rid of the seeds. Fill the lolly moulds, then add the sticks and freeze.

berry nice lollies

Enjoy hot days licking
very cool ice lollies!

You will need:

125 g (4 oz) raspberries

raspberries

juice of 2
medium
oranges

60 ml
(2 fl oz) water

40 g (1 ½ oz)
caster sugar

zoom!

150 g (5 oz)
strawberries, hulled
and cut in half

How to make them...

1 **Boil the sugar** and water in a pan. Stir constantly until the sugar is dissolved.

2 **Puree and sieve** the strawberries and raspberries. Mix with the sugary water and orange juice.

3 **Pour the mixture** into ice lolly moulds. Pop in the sticks and freeze until solid.

chocolate sundae

Here's a sweet treat that couldn't be easier to make.

You will need:

2 chocolate muffins

3 tbsp single cream

2 scoops vanilla ice cream

60 g (2 oz) chocolate caramel bar

1 **Melt the caramel** bar in a bowl set over a pan of hot water. Add the cream and stir to make a smooth sauce.

2 **Scoop out** the tops of the muffins. Spoon on the vanilla ice cream, then pour on the caramel sauce and enjoy!

strawberry cream surprise

This no-cook pud is crunchy and smooth – and deliciously sweet.

You will need:
4 small scoops of strawberry ice cream

sprigs of mint

2 meringue shells

200 g (7 oz) strawberries

1 Break meringue into small pieces. Hull the strawberries. Mash half of them and slice the rest.

2 Fill two glasses with layers of mashed and sliced strawberries, ice cream, and meringue pieces.

3 Finish off with a spoonful of ice cream and mashed strawberries. Decorate each glass with a sprig of mint, then serve.

Index

Annabel Karmel is a leading author on cooking for children and has written 12 best-selling books which are sold all over the world.

She is an expert in devising tasty and nutritious meals for children without the need for parents to spend hours in the kitchen.

Annabel writes regularly for National newspapers including *The Times* and the *Daily Mail* and appears frequently on radio and television as the UK's expert on children's nutritional issues.

Thank you

Acknowledgments

With thanks to the children who took part in the photography:

Arabella Earley (MOT Junior Agency), Emily Wigoder, Euan Thomson, and Harry Holmstoel (Norrie Carr Agency).

Thanks also to Penny Arlon, Penny Smith, and Wendy Bartlet for editorial and design work on this book.

annabel karmel

Visit Annabel's website
www.annabelkarmel.com

Scones

3 cups S.R. Flour

1 cup Milk

1 cup cream single

1 teaspoon Sugar (

mix w. Fork loosely

Floured Surface + flour on top

pat down 1" thick

Cut out Scones (glass etc)

leftovers re form etc

200°c 13 mins